SUNNYSIDE
PRIMARY SCHOOL

Our World
Wind Energy

By Rob Bowden

Aladdin/Watts
London • Sydney

© Aladdin Books Ltd 2006

Designed and produced by
Aladdin Books Ltd
2/3 Fitzroy Mews
London W1T 6DF

First published in 2006 by
Franklin Watts
338 Euston Road
London NW1 3BH

Franklin Watts Australia
Hachette Children's Books
Level 17/207 Kent Street
Sydney NSW 2000

A catalogue record for this
book is available from the
British Library.

Dewey Classification: 333.9'2

ISBN 0 7496 6826 1

Printed in Malaysia

All rights reserved

Editor:
Harriet Brown

Designer:
Flick, Book Design and Graphics

Consultant:
Jackie Holderness – former Senior Lecturer
in Primary Education, Westminster Institute,
Oxford Brookes University

Picture researcher:
Alexa Brown

Photocredits:
Abbreviations: l-left, r-right, b-bottom, t-top, c-centre,
m-middle. Front cover – US Department of Energy. Back
cover – Corbis. 23bl – Cassop Primary School, 12tl –
Comstock, 29tr - Conceptual architectural design for
WEB 'Multi-Turbine Twin Tower' Building"; Institut für
Baukonstruktion und Entwerfen L2, University of
Stuttgart; Project WEB - Wind Energy for the Built
Environment [EC JOR3-CT98-0270], web@bdsp.com
and www.bdsp.com, 6tl, 8br – Corbis, 2-3, 5ml, 18tl,
18br, 19tr, 19ml, 19bl, 19br, 30mr - Elsam, 4bl, 14br,
24tr - © EWEA / Winter, 27tr – John Foxx Images, 16tl –
21t – Norio Cubo, 3tl, 6m, 11bl – Photodisc, 5tl, 9tl,
30tr – The Poul la Cour Museum, www.poullacour.dk,
25br – Rob Bowden, EASI-Educational Resources, 22ml
– Swaffham, www.ecotricity.com, 29br – Skysails, 24bl
– TongRo, 3mbl, 7tr, 9br, 13tl, 13br, 14tl, 15tr, 15bl,
22tr, 25tl, 26br, 28tl, 28br – US Department of Energy,
23tr – WindSave Ltd, 5br, 31bl, 12br, 17tr –
www.istockphoto.com, 10tl – www.istockphoto.com /
Anke Holwerde, 5tr, 17bl, 31t - www.istockphoto.com
/ Laurie Knight, 3mtl, 8tl – www.istockphoto.com / Lise
Gagne, 1, 3bl, 5bl, 26tl, 27bl, 30br –
www.istockphoto.com / Malcolm Romain,
www.istockphoto.com / Paul Wilkinson,
www.istockphoto.com / Rasmus Rasmussen, 10br –
www.istockphoto.com / Rob Sylvan, 4ml –
www.istockphoto.com / William Fawcett

CONTENTS

Notes to parents and teachers

This series has been developed for group use in the classroom as well as for children reading on their own. In particular, its differentiated text allows children of mixed abilities to enjoy reading about the same topic. The larger size text (A, below) offers apprentice readers a simplified text. This simplified text is used in the introduction to each chapter and in the picture captions. This font is part of the © Sassoon family of fonts recommended by the National Literacy Early Years Strategy document for maximum legibility. The smaller size text (B, below) offers a more challenging read for older or more able readers.

A modern turbine

The blades of a modern wind turbine can be over 40 metres long and stand on a tower 80 metres high.

A

◄ **The blades are attached to the nacelle.**

Modern wind turbines are very different from the early windmills.

B

Questions, key words and glossary

Each spread ends with a question which parents and teachers can use to discuss and develop further ideas and concepts. Further questions are provided in a quiz on page 30. A reduced version of pages 30 and 31 is shown below. The illustrated 'Key words' section is provided as a revision tool, particularly for apprentice readers, in order to help with spelling, writing and guided reading as part of the literacy hour. The glossary is for more able or older readers. In addition to the glossary's role as a reference aid, it is also designed to reinforce new vocabulary and provide a tool for further discussion and revision. When glossary terms first appear in the text they are highlighted in bold.

 See how much you know!

What is wind energy?

How are winds formed?

When was the first electricity producing wind turbine built?

How do people use the wind's energy?

Where is the best place to put a wind farm?

How does offshore wind power work?

What are the benefits of wind power?

Why do some people complain about wind power?

What are the disadvantages of wind power?

Key words

Anemometer

A

**Generator
Meteorologist
Power
Rotor blade
Windmill**

Turbine

Glossary

Atmosphere – The mixture of gases that surrounds the Earth.
Hemisphere – Half of a sphere. The Equator divides the Earth into the Northern and Southern hemispheres.
Meteorologist – A scientist who measures and studies the climate.
Nacelle – The name given to the part of a wind turbine that contains the gears and the generator.
Tail wind – Any strong wind that pushes from behind.

B

Transformer – A device that changes the way electricity is sent.
Turbulent – When wind is gusty and blows unevenly it is turbulent. A steady wind has less turbulence.
Yaw mechanism – A system of electronics and cogs that turn the turbine to face into the wind.

What is wind?

Wind is the movement of air in the atmosphere from one place to another. Wind can move at different speeds and strengths. Wind can be warm or cold. The movement of the wind makes the clouds move and changes the weather.

 These rain clouds are blown by the wind.

The Earth's **atmosphere** is made up of areas of high and low pressure. These are caused by differences in the temperature of the air and the Earth's surface. Areas of high pressure push air towards areas of lower pressure. This movement of air is what we call wind.

This weather scientist (meteorologist) uses a floating balloon to measure the wind.

Meteorologists study winds around the world. The trade winds blow towards the Equator from the north-east in the Northern **hemisphere** and the south-east in the Southern hemisphere. Where these winds meet around the Equator, there is an area of low pressure and gentle winds called the doldrums. The Westerlies are also trade winds flowing west to east.

Monsoon winds blow across southern Asia. They are powerful and bring heavy rainfall. In India, farmers rely on the monsoon winds and rain for their crops.

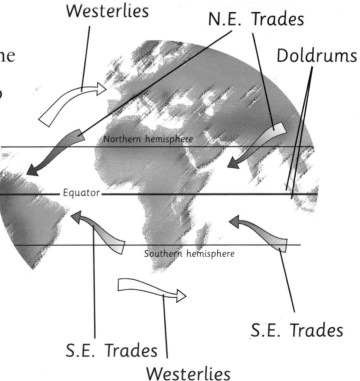

Westerlies   N.E. Trades

Doldrums

Northern hemisphere

Equator

Southern hemisphere

S.E. Trades

S.E. Trades

Westerlies

 What is the strongest wind you can remember?

What is wind energy?

Have you ever had your hat blown off by the wind? Has a strong gust of wind ever made you lose your balance? If so, then you have experienced the energy of the wind. People have used the wind's energy for thousands of years.

▶ This boat uses sails to catch the wind's energy.

The earliest human use of wind energy was for sail-boats. The ancient Egyptians used sails to catch the wind and move boats along the River Nile around 6,000 years ago. The first windmills were made in Persia (now Iran) around 1,400 years ago. Windmills and wind turbines use the wind's energy to turn machinery. Windmills grind grain or pump water. Today, wind turbines create electricity.

◀ **This early wind turbine, built in 1897, made electricity from the wind's energy.**

In 1887, the first wind turbine was built for generating electricity. It was not very efficient. A Danish man called Poul la Cour improved the design in 1897. By 1918, Denmark had enough wind turbines to produce around three per cent of the country's electricity.

A wind farm uses giant turbines to turn the wind's energy into electricity.

Today, the wind is mainly used to generate electricity known as wind power. The energy of the wind is collected by a wind turbine and converted into electricity for use in homes, businesses and schools. Wind turbines are normally built in clusters known as wind farms.

 Can you think of other examples of using wind energy?

Powerful wind

Wind energy plays an important part in the natural world. Seeds are carried by the wind to land where they grow into new plants. Birds use wind energy to help them travel over long distances. Wind energy also causes damage. It blows over trees, and brings huge waves and storms.

These geese are pushed along by strong winds called tail winds. ▼

Some birds use the energy of the wind. It helps them travel long distances when they migrate from one country to another. Birds find strong winds that push them along. This saves them having to beat their wings as often. These winds are called **tail winds**. Aircraft also use tail winds to push them along.

▶ This kite is lifted by the wind's energy.

The wind's energy can help aeroplanes to reach their destinations more quickly. A wind called the jet stream blows high above the Earth's surface. If an aeroplane flies in the same direction as the jet stream, it acts as a tail wind. A journey across the Atlantic Ocean takes around one hour less than if the aeroplane flies against the jet stream.

The winds of a tropical cyclone cause great damage.

Tropical cyclones (also called hurricanes or typhoons) are some of the most powerful winds on Earth. They can have winds that travel up to 350 km/hour. Most hurricanes stay at sea, but some come ashore. Their winds destroy buildings and power lines. Hurricanes, such as the one that hit New Orleans in 2005, can cause widespread flooding.

 In what ways does the wind help or harm nature?

How does wind power work?

Wind is created when energy from the Sun heats up the air around you. Of all the Sun's energy that reaches the Earth, around one or two per cent is changed into wind energy. This is an enormous amount of energy. For us to use it, it must be captured and turned into power.

▲ ▶ **The Sun creates wind energy that turns rotor blades.**

Wind power uses the energy of the wind to turn rotor blades. The rotor blades are connected to a generator that produces electricity. The electricity is carried along wires to our homes and schools, and to shops and offices.

◀ Rotor blades catch the wind's energy as it blows through them.

Wind turbines use giant rotor blades to catch the wind's energy. The turbine is located at the top of a tower behind the rotor blades. Gears increase the energy delivered by the blades and transfer it to a generator. The generator produces electricity.

Rotor blades are many times bigger than an average person.

The power produced by a wind turbine depends on the size of the rotor blades and on the wind speed. The bigger the rotor blades and the stronger the wind, the more power the turbine will generate. The design of wind turbines and their locations are therefore very important. At the moment, less than one per cent of the world's electricity comes from wind power.

 Where would be a good location for a wind farm?

A modern wind turbine

The blades of a modern wind turbine can be over 40 metres long and stand on a tower 80 metres high. In good winds, they can generate enough electricity to supply around 900 typical European homes.

► **The blades are attached to the nacelle. Inside the nacelle is the generator.**

Modern wind turbines are very different from the early windmills. They are now made out of modern materials and controlled by electronics and computers. The main parts of a turbine are the tower, the **nacelle** and the rotor blades. The rotor blades are connected to the front of the nacelle and the whole lot sits on top of a tower.

► Rotor blades are made to be lightweight but strong.

Most wind turbines have three rotor blades. The rotor blades have an aerodynamic shape (like an aeroplane wing) that helps them to catch as much wind energy as possible. Modern blades are made from materials such as carbon fibre, glass fibre and polyester. These materials allow the blade to bend a little in the wind without breaking.

Steel tubes are bolted together to make a wind tower taller than four houses!

The tower of a wind turbine is normally a steel tube that is bolted to a concrete base. The tube is made in sections and transported to the tower site on large lorries. Cranes lift the sections into place and they are bolted together to form the tower.

 Why do you think wind towers need to be tall?

Where to locate a wind farm

A wind turbine needs a reliable supply of wind to generate electricity. The best land-based places for a wind farm are on coasts and areas of high ground.

▶ Wind farms are built in windy places, such as on top of a hill.

More than half of the wind energy hitting a modern turbine can be converted into electricity, but only if the turbine is in the right location. The best locations are those with a regular wind and no obstacles to block the wind from reaching the rotor blades. This is why wind turbines are located on hills, cliffs or in a location where the wind is not blocked by any buildings.

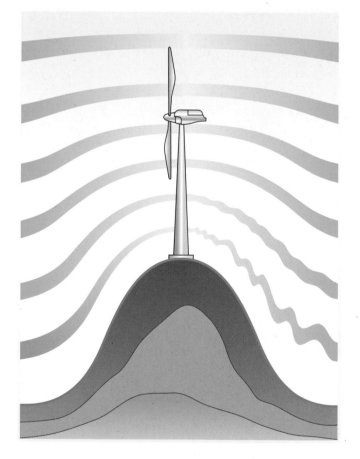

▶ The wind vane on top of the nacelle measures the direction of the wind.

To generate as much power as possible, a wind turbine must face into the wind. The wind vane sends signals to a **yaw mechanism**. The yaw mechanism uses a system of cogs to turn the nacelle and rotor blades into the wind.

An anemometer measures the speed of the wind.

The speed of the wind is very important for wind farms. If the wind is too slow, then the turbines will not work. If it is too fast, then they will shut down to avoid being damaged. Most turbines work in wind speeds of between 18 and 90 km/hour. An anemometer measures the wind speed and can automatically turn the turbine on or off as required.

 Where else are cogs used to turn wheels?

Offshore wind power

Wind farms can be built offshore (out at sea). There is more wind energy at sea than there is on land. The electricity the farms produce is sent back to the land along underwater cables.

► **These homes use electricity generated by offshore wind power.**

One of the most reliable places for wind is at sea. There are few obstacles at sea so the wind is smoother and less **turbulent** than on land. The first offshore wind farm in the USA could begin generating electricity in 2009. It is called the Cape Wind Project. If it is built, it will be located in Nantucket Sound off Cape Cod in Massachusetts.

Offshore wind farms are built using special equipment.

Calm weather is needed to build offshore wind farms. Only shallow coastal waters are suitable for offshore wind farms. In the future, floating and deeper-water wind farms may become possible.

(1) Radar is used to help decide where to position the steel piles.

(2) The steel piles are driven into the sea bed to support the turbine. The piles are coated with specialised resins and paint to stop them rusting, and painted brightly so that ships can easily see them.

(3) The nacelle and rotor blades are placed on top of the steel piles.

(4) The turbine is linked by underwater cables to an offshore **transformer**. Divers are used to install the cables. A cable carries the electricity from the transformer back to shore.

What problems might happen on offshore wind farms?

Who uses wind power?

Over 50 countries use wind power to generate electricity. Around 72 per cent of the world's wind power is produced in Europe. Roughly 18 per cent of the world's wind power is produced in the USA. The use of wind power is increasing.

► **Many countries are now building giant wind farms to make electricity.**

Germany and Spain are by far the world leaders in wind power production, but Denmark is the country that most relies on wind power. In 2004, wind power provided 19 per cent of Denmark's electricity. India and China are rapidly developing wind farms.

Wind power is growing very quickly across the world.

The use of wind power more than doubled between 2000 and 2004. It is one of the fastest growing types of energy, but it only produced less than one per cent of the world's electricity in 2002. The wind power industry plans to produce 12 per cent of the world's electricity by 2020.

The use of wind power in megawatts (MW) per year:

2004
47,912 MW

2000
18,449 MW

1996
6,104 MW

1992
2,321 MW

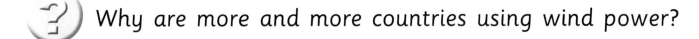

Why are more and more countries using wind power?

Local wind power

Wind power can be used locally to power individual houses or schools. It is especially good in remote areas away from other power sources. Some caravans and boats also use wind power to provide electricity.

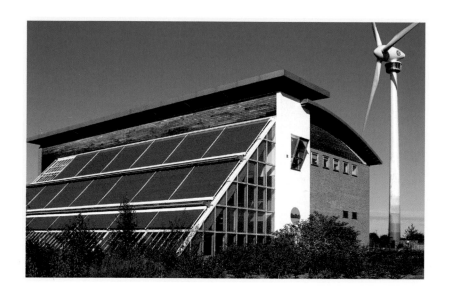

◀ **This wind turbine is being used to provide electricity for this education centre.**

Small-scale wind turbines can provide electricity at a local level and are now used across the world. Once installed, wind turbines need little maintenance or expertise and will last many years. In most cases wind power is used with other types of energy such as solar energy. Solar energy is captured by solar panels and is turned into electricity.

▶ This house has a tiny turbine that is used to generate electricity.

Very small wind turbines are called micro-turbines. They can be used to charge batteries and provide electricity for houses, caravans or boats. They are better to use than diesel or petrol generators as they are less noisy and produce no pollution.

This school uses wind power as an environmentally-friendly source of electricity.

Wind power can be used locally even if you are not in a remote location. In the UK, Cassop primary school in County Durham has a wind turbine in its grounds. The turbine produces about twice the electricity needed by the school. The extra electricity is sold to electricity companies to be used elsewhere.

Why is wind power a clean source of energy?

The benefits of wind power

Wind is a free and endless supply of energy. Once they are built, wind turbines offer clean energy with no pollution. Wind power is a good alternative to burning fossil fuels, such as coal.

◄ **There is enough wind energy available to meet all of our power needs.**

The wind is a renewable source of energy, which means it will never run out. There is more wind energy available than we will ever need. Wind energy is also a clean energy that produces no pollution once the turbine is built and installed.

▲ Wind power has created many new jobs.

Wind power creates many jobs for people making, installing and operating the wind turbines. In 2004, there were over 100,000 people involved in the wind power industry worldwide. Wind power is also cheaper than solar power or nuclear power and about the same cost as power generated from coal.

Wind power can help to improve people's quality of life.

Wind power can be used in remote regions where other types of energy are not available. Wind power can give remote villages electricity for lighting or for pumping water. In Wales, small wind turbines are even being used to run telephones (below).

 What makes wind power a good form of energy?

Arguments against wind power

Some people think that wind turbines spoil the landscape. They also say that wind farms are harmful to wildlife and that they are too noisy if they are built too close to where people live.

► **Do you think that wind farms spoil the beauty of the countryside?**

Wind farms are often built in rural landscapes where there are no other buildings. Because some people think that they spoil the landscape, some think that one solution is to build more offshore wind farms because fewer people would see them.

Wind farms are blamed for killing birds.

Wind farms have been blamed for disturbing wildlife. Some studies suggest that birds, such as eagles, are killed by flying into the giant rotor blades. Other studies suggest that this is not true and that most birds fly over or around them. Before a new wind farm is built, studies are carried out to assess the danger to wildlife.

Some people say wind farms are noisy.

If you stand near a wind turbine you will hear the noise of its rotor blades spinning in the wind. Some people complain that this noise disturbs people living nearby. However, most wind farms are built at least 300 metres from homes. At this distance the noise is less than that of a car engine.

How would you feel if a wind farm was built near your house?

The future of wind power

Wind power will be more important in the future with more wind farms and more powerful turbines. Tall buildings may be designed to catch wind energy and generate electricity. Wind power is also being used to create energy for cars.

▶ **These massive wind turbines are in the USA.**

Wind turbines are getting bigger and more powerful every year. A typical 1.8 MW (megawatt) turbine will produce enough electricity in a year to meet the power needs of 1,000 homes. New wind turbines now being built are 5 MW or bigger, and this means they will make an even bigger contribution to world energy supplies in the future.

▶ This building would generate its own wind power.

Some architects have designed buildings that have wind turbines built into their design. These tall buildings could capture wind energy in towns and cities. They could produce at least 20 per cent of their own energy needs. Boat builders have also designed boats that are powered using wind turbines instead of sails.

In the future, wind energy may be used to pull cargo ships.

A German company called SkySails is developing an enormous 'kite' that flies at 500 metres above the ship. If it is used to help pull cargo ships, it could massively reduce the amount of diesel consumed.

 Why should we use more wind power in the future?

See how much you know!

What is wind energy?

How are winds formed?

When was the first electricity producing wind turbine built?

How do people use the wind's energy?

Where is the best place to put a wind farm?

How does offshore wind power work?

What are the benefits of wind power?

Why do some people complain about wind power?

What are the disadvantages of wind power?

Key words

Anemometer

Energy supply

Generator

Meteorologist

Power

Rotor blade

Windmill

Turbine

Glossary

Atmosphere – The mixture of gases that surrounds the Earth.

Hemisphere – Half of a sphere. The Equator divides the Earth into the Northern and Southern hemispheres.

Meteorologist – A scientist who measures and studies the climate.

Nacelle – The name given to the part of a wind turbine that contains the gears and the generator.

Tail wind – Any strong wind that pushes from behind.

Transformer – A device that changes the way electricity is sent.

Turbulent – When wind is gusty and blows unevenly it is turbulent. A steady wind has less turbulence.

Yaw mechanism – A system of electronics and cogs that turn the nacelle of the turbine to face into the wind.

Index